MANCHESTER
CITY COUNCIL

2 4 AUG 2023

- 3 FEB 2024

1 7 FEB 2024

Please return/renew this item
by the last date shown.
Books may also be renewed by
phone or the internet.

Tel: 0161 254 7777

www.manchester.gov.uk/libraries

Written by Clive Gifford
Illustrations by Emiliano Migliardo

Cover typography based on designs by Thy Bui.

First published in Great Britain in 2023 by Red Shed, part of Farshore

An imprint of HarperCollins*Publishers*
1 London Bridge Street, London SE1 9GF
www.farshore.co.uk

HarperCollins*Publishers*
Macken House, 39/40 Mayor Street Upper
Dublin 1, D01 C9W8

ISBN 978 0 00 861574 1

Printed and bound in the UK using 100% renewable
electricity at CPI Group (UK) Ltd

001

A CIP catalogue record for this title is available from the British Library.

Stay safe online. Any website addresses listed in this book are correct at the time of going
to print. However, Farshore is not responsible for content hosted by third parties. Please be
aware that online content can be subject to change and websites can contain content that is
unsuitable for children. We advise that all children are supervised when using the internet.

This book is produced from independently certified FSC™ paper
to ensure responsible forest management.

For more information visit: www.harpercollins.co.uk/green

AMAZING F⚽OTBALL FACTS

FOR EVERY 7 YEAR OLD

RED SHED

If you love watching or playing football, you'll find **TONS** of fascinating facts in this fun-filled book . . .

Which football club was sold for just £1?

Where in the world is tractor football played?

How old was the youngest person to be signed by a football club?

Read on to find out the answers and lots more awesome information about the beautiful game . . .

The world's largest football is 12.19 metres across and weighs an incredible 960 kilograms – about the weight of three adult horses.

It was unveiled by the Doha Bank in Qatar, United Arab Emirates, in 2013.

Danish referee Henning Erikstrup's false teeth fell out when he went to blow the final whistle in a 1960 match.

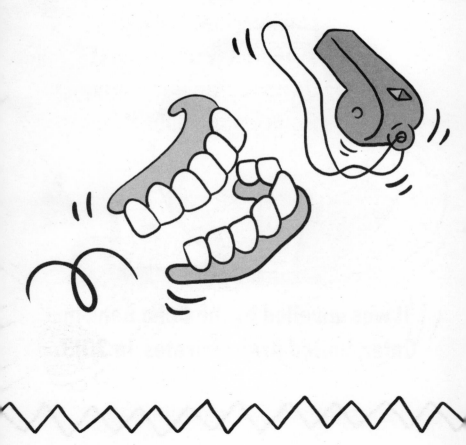

In a match between France
and Switzerland during
EURO 2016, the football burst
when Swiss midfielder Valon
Behrami went to kick it.

Japanese teenager Misaki Murakami lost his football when it got washed away in a 2011 tsunami. It ended up on the shores of Alaska a year later.

Only a handful of countries in the world, like the US and Canada, call football 'soccer'.

However, the word 'soccer' actually originated in Britain!

'Soccer' was short for 'assoccer' which was short for 'association football'. The British stopped using the word over 40 years ago in favour of 'football'.

In the first ever FIFA World Cup final in 1930, Belgian referee John Langenus wore a dinner suit jacket with a red striped tie and knickerbocker trousers!

Nicole Petignat from Switzerland became the first female referee to take charge of a UEFA Cup match when she officiated the game between a Swedish and Icelandic club in 2003.

Italian striker Fernando d'Ercoli was shown a red card by the referee during a 1989 match and got so angry that he grabbed the card and ate it!

Hull City Football Club celebrated reaching the 2014 FA Cup final by selling unusual objects to fans, like a toilet seat in black and gold (the club colours) with manager Steve Bruce's face under the lid!

Wembley Stadium in London has 2,618 toilets – more than any other stadium in the world.

The FIFA World Cup trophy is made of 18 carat gold with a malachite base. It is hollow instead of solid, otherwise it would be too heavy for the winners to lift!

At just six millimetres tall, the
Lyonesse Cup is the world's
smallest football trophy.

The world's largest football trophy
is the Costa del Sol trophy, which
stands at around 1.2 metres –
almost as tall as you!

England won their first Women's EURO in 2022, beating opponents Germany 2-1 in the final.

Brazilian teenager Aldyr Garcia Schlee won a competition to design Brazil's new football kit in the 1950s. His design of a gold shirt with blue shorts, white socks and green and gold trim is still worn today!

In the 2012 Coupe de France final, the Olympique Lyonnais team wore football shirts with a strip that could only be seen by viewers wearing 3D glasses – a first in football history!

As Greek defender Sokratis Papastathopoulos's surname is too long to be printed on his football shirt, his first name is printed instead.

The world's largest football shirt was unveiled in Lagos, Nigeria, in 2013.

At 73.55 metres wide and 89.67 metres long, it took up almost all of the city's Teslim Balogun stadium!

The fastest free kick ever recorded reached a speed of 211 kilometres per hour – faster than the top speed of most cars!

When Zaire (now the Democratic
Republic of the Congo) qualified
for the 1974 World Cup, President
Mobutu Sese Seko gifted each player
a house and a green Volkswagen car.

While World Cup mascots are often based on animals, the mascot for the 1982 World Cup, held in Spain, was an orange called Naranjito.

The mascot for English team Wigan Athletic is a pie called Crusty.

One of the mascots for English team West Bromwich is called Boiler Man.

Leganés Sports Club in Spain have a mascot called Super Cucumber, who wears a superhero mask and cape!

The youngest person to be signed by a football club is Bryce Brites in 2013. He was signed to Belgium's Racing Boxberg team at just 20 months (under two years) old.

Samuel Keplinger from Germany refereed a local boys' football match when he was just nine years and 302 days old, making him the youngest known football referee.

Striker Monica Quinteros launched her football career for the Ecuador national women's team at 13 years old. She later helped them qualify for their first Women's World Cup in 2015.

Brazilian footballer Ronaldinho played for a local team in Porto Alegre when he was 13 years old. The team won a match 23–0, and all 23 goals were scored by Ronaldinho!

The youngest ever World Cup coach is Vanessa Arauz. She coached the Ecuador team in the 2015 Women's World Cup at 26 years old.

Otto Rehhagel was 71 years old when he coached the Greek national team during the 2010 World Cup, making him the oldest World Cup coach in history.

Peter Pak-Ngo Pang entered record books in 2013 as the oldest ever referee. He was 80 years and 161 days old!

Eric Godpower Marshall, who plays
for Gar'ou Football Club in Liberia,
was named the youngest ever person
to play at official senior level by his
club when he was 11 years old.

Brazilian farmer Tercio Mariano de Rezende loved football so much that, in 2008, he was still playing for his home town club at the age of 87!

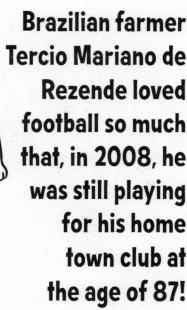

Football five-a-side, featuring blind or partially sighted players, became a Paralympic sport at the Games in Athens in 2004. The team from Brazil has won gold at every Paralympics so far.

Players wear eyeshades during games. However, the goalkeeper can be sighted or partially sighted.

There must be complete silence during games to allow the players to hear the ball, which has a bell inside. Fans, players and their coaches must be quiet . . . until a goal is scored!

Players say "voy" to let others know when they are going in for a tackle.

Every Christmas Eve, approximately 20,000 fans of German football club Union Berlin sing Christmas carols at their home ground.

Every time Canadian football club
Montreal Impact score a goal during
a home game, the fans ring a giant bell
called North Star!

Fans of the Rapid Vienna football
team clap their hands fast for the last
15 minutes of a match.

Lionesses star Beth Mead has an octopus named after her. Staff at the Sea Life in Scarborough, UK, chose the name to celebrate the Lionesses' historic win in the UEFA Women's EURO 2022.

32 Bayern Munich fans couldn't get tickets to their team's UEFA Champions League match against CSKA Moscow in 2014, so they rented the 18th floor of an office building overlooking the grounds to watch!

In 2016, after setting a new Italian record for not letting any goals in, goalkeeper Gianluigi Buffon wrote a love letter to the goal he protects during matches.

**Welsh goalkeeper
Leigh Richmond Roose would often
perform gymnastics using the goal's
crossbar during breaks in play!**

Icelandic football club Stjarnan are known for their humorous goal celebrations. As well as imitating catching a fish with a fishing pole, the players have formed a human bicycle and a human toilet!

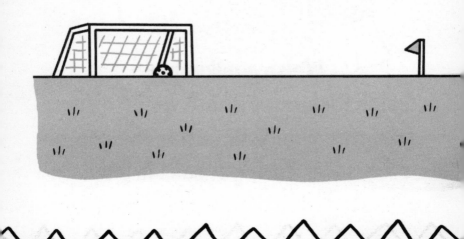

Pierre-Emerick Aubameyang from France loves superheroes, and sometimes celebrates his goals by pulling a superhero mask from his sock and wearing it!

In 2014, Belarussian striker Dzimtry Koub celebrated one of his goals by running off the pitch, climbing into the stands and sitting in an empty seat to applaud himself.

Manchester City's Bernardo Corradi celebrated his goal against Fulham in 2006 by 'knighting' teammate Joey Barton with the corner flag.

At the 1998 World Cup, French defender Laurent Blanc kissed the bald head of his teammate, goalkeeper Fabien Barthez, as a pre-match ritual. It must have worked as France won the tournament!

German attacker Marco Reus always puts his right boot on first and steps on to the pitch with his right foot, then hops two times before he plays.

Before any game, Romanian striker-now-manager Adrian Mutu would stuff basil leaves in his football socks and wear his match underpants inside-out for good luck!

And it's not just players who have football match rituals. Fans of Spanish club Deportivo de la Coruña sprinkle cloves of garlic onto the pitch before every game to keep bad luck away.

Romeo Anconetani, president of Italian club Pisa during the 1980s and early 1990s, threw salt onto the pitch before every home game for good luck. The more important the game, the more salt he threw.

The first World Cup tournament took place in Uruguay, South America, in 1930.

The biggest World Cup score is 31–0, won by Australia in their 2002 qualifying game against American Samoa.

The first Women's World Cup was held in China in 1991.

Canada's Janine Beckie scored the fastest goal ever in Olympic women's football in 2016 – just 20 seconds after kick-off.

The fastest goal in Olympic men's football was scored by Mexico's Oribe Peralta, 29 seconds after the start of the 2012 final against Brazil.

Portuguese football star Cristiano Ronaldo is one of the richest footballers in the world.

He became the all-time male international record scorer in 2021 and has scored over 115 goals for Portugal.

Five of these goals came at EURO 2020, where Ronaldo also became the first footballer to appear at five EURO tournaments.

The University of British Columbia in Canada offers a course that teaches students about Ronaldo and his impact on society.

The first world championship for table football players took place in Denver, USA, in 1975.

The biggest table football table, unveiled in Italy in 2015, measured 121.4 metres long. It had handles for up to 424 players.

The world record for the most football headers while treading water is 1,644 – held by Jhoen Lefont Rodríguez from Cuba!

The world record for the most touches of a football while hanging from a lamppost is 219, set by Algerian freestyle footballer Abdellah Belabbas in 2013.

Uruguay defender José Batista was sent off just 56 seconds after a 1986 World Cup game between Uruguay and Belgium had started – a World Cup record to this day!

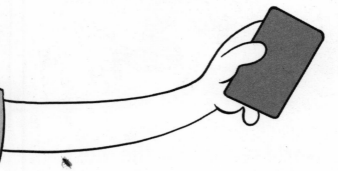

A red card is given when a player commits a serious offence or books two yellow cards in the same game. They are sent off the pitch and not replaced.

In 1914, fans at the El Morro stadium in Chile saw what is thought to be football's first ever bicycle kick, performed by 20-year-old forward Ramón Unzaga Asla.

Australia's Ellyse Perry is the first player ever to have appeared in a cricket World Cup (2009) and a football World Cup (2011).

Striker Robbie Keane from the Republic of Ireland is the only player in the world to have scored at least one international goal every season for 18 seasons in a row (1998–2016).

The record number of attempted passes made in a single game is 934, set by Barcelona Football Club – 840 were completed successfully.

Brazilian forward Marta Vieira da Silva was voted the world's best female footballer six times. Her first win in 2006, when she was 20 years old, made her the youngest recipient.

Former French attacking midfielder Zinedine Zidane was voted world's best male footballer three times.

Legendary striker Pelé was born Edson Arantes do Nascimento in 1940.

He scored over 1,200 goals for his club, Santos, and a further 77 for the Brazilian national team.

He scored 93 hat-tricks in total, and four goals in a single game on 31 different occasions!

The 1958 World Cup, hosted by Sweden, saw Pelé become the youngest ever goal scorer and World Cup winner at 17 years and 249 days old.

Seating 114,000 people, the Rungrado 1st of May Stadium in Pyongyang, North Korea, is the largest football stadium in the world.

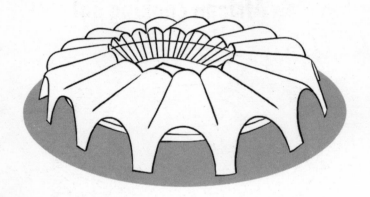

The highest stadium in the world is the Estadio Daniel Alcides Carrión in Pasco, Peru. It is perched 4,380 metres above sea level – around half the height of Mount Everest!

The FNB Stadium in Johannesburg, South Africa, is nicknamed 'The Calabash', as the multi-coloured, tiled outer surface looks like an African cooking pot.

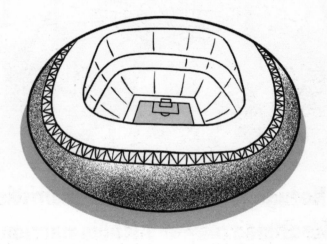

It is also the largest stadium on the African continent, with a capacity of 94,736.

Norwegian football club Tromsø Idrettslag play at a stadium deep within the Arctic Circle, and is the most northerly professional club in the world.

The most southerly top football club in the world is Southern United in New Zealand.

Monaco's stadium, Stade Louis II, has enough seats for more than half of the country's entire population.

The Ottmar Hizfield stadium in Switzerland is so high up in the mountains that it can only be reached by cable car!

The Evergrande Football School in China – the largest residential football school in the world – has a 13-metre-tall sculpture of the FIFA World Cup trophy. That's about the same as three double-decker buses stacked on top of each other!

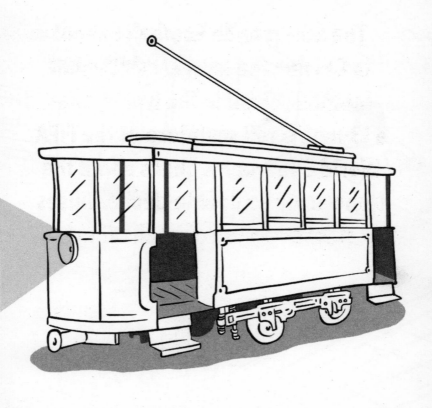

The first ever floodlit match in Brazil was played in 1923 on a pitch lit up by tram headlights.

The Unusual Football Pitch Project squeezes odd-shaped football pitches into cramped spaces in built-up deprived areas of Bangkok, Thailand. Some pitches even go round corners!

In 2005, an important World Cup qualifying game held in Nairobi between Kenya and Morocco was interrupted by a massive Marabou stork.

An Australian youth football game in 2016 was interrupted by a bull charging across the pitch. It chased players before escaping through a gap in the fence.

Four divers with tanks and masks took part in an underwater football match inside a fish aquarium in China to mark the 2014 World Cup.

The 2022 World Cup in Qatar was the first to take place during November and December – winter in the northern hemisphere.

The World Cup usually takes place in June and July when temperatures in Qatar can reach over 45 degrees Celsius!

Qatar was the smallest nation ever to host the FIFA World Cup, and the first in the Middle East to do so.

The Brazilian national team is the only side that has appeared in every FIFA World Cup, and they have won the tournament five times – more than any other team.

Dick, Kerr Ladies was one of England's earliest-known teams in women's association football. They had a huge following, and 25,000 fans watched them beat a French team 2–0 in a 1920 match.

Women's football was incredibly popular, with Lily Parr and Alice Kell being star players. But the English Football Association (FA) banned women's football games in 1921. The ban was finally lifted in 1971.

NO WOMEN ALLOWED

The oldest surviving continental football competition is the Copa América, which began in 1916 (44 years before the UEFA European Championships).

Uruguay and Argentina have won the competition 15 times each!

The world's oldest surviving club is Sheffield Football Club, which was founded in 1857.
It's been around longer than electric lightbulbs have!

Bossaball is a hybrid of football, volleyball and trampolining.

Tractor football matches take place using a special two-metre-wide football at the National Ploughing Championships in Ireland.

Bubble soccer was invented in Oslo, Norway, in 2011.

There is such a thing as three-sided football! The game is played with three teams instead of two, and the pitch is hexagon-shaped.

In FootGolf, players have to kick a regular-sized football into an oversized golf hole in as few kicks as possible.

Icelandic Mud Football is a six-a-side game played in . . . mud. Pushing and pulling are part of the game!

A small museum in Argentina devoted to footballs had a record number of over 861 footballs from all around the globe in 2005.

Letchworth Albion Football Club was sold online for just £45 in 2014!

The first European Championships, held in France in 1960, cost national teams 100 Swiss Francs (about £388 today) to enter. In 2020, teams received a minimum of 9.25 million Euros (just over £8.1 million).

That year, tournament winners Italy were awarded a whopping 34 million Euros (almost £30 million).

In 2002, Norwegian striker Kenneth Kristensen was bought by a football club for his weight in prawns – 75 kilograms.

In 1982, businessman Ken Bates bought Chelsea FC for just £1.

He sold it on to Roman Abramovich in 2003 for £140 million!

In 2016, Zhang Shuang from China managed to race 50 metres with a football held between his legs while walking on his hands!

NASL Soccer, released by Mattel Electronics in 1979, was the first football computer game that had moving players and some of the rules of the real sport.

Look out for other books in the series!